SPALDING "
ATH:

MW00454435

SCIENTIFIC PHYSICAL TRAINING
SERIES

INDIAN CLUB EXERCISES

BY

EDWARD B. WARMAN

LOS ANGELES, CALIFORNIA

Author of The Care of the Body. Physical Training
Simplified. The Voice—How to Train It, How to
Care for It; Gestures and Attitudes; Delsarte
Philosophy of Expression. How to Read,
Recite and Impersonate. Practical
Orthoepy and Critique.

Copyright © 2013 Read Books Ltd.
This book is copyright and may not be
reproduced or copied in any way without
the express permission of the publisher in writing

British Library Cataloguing-in-Publication Data
A catalogue record for this book is available from the
British Library

Indian Clubs

'Indian clubs', or 'Iranian clubs' belong to a category of exercise equipment used for developing strength, and in juggling. In appearance, they resemble elongated bowling-pins, and are commonly made out of wood. They come in all shapes and sizes however, ranging from a few pounds each, to fifty pounds, and are commonly swung in certain patterns as part of exercise programs. They were often used in class formats, predominantly in Iran, where members would perform choreographed routines, led by an instructor; remarkably similar to modern aerobics classes. Despite their name, 'Indian clubs' actually originated in ancient Persia, Egypt and the Middle East, where they were used by wrestlers. The practice has continued to the present day, notably in the varzesh-e bastani tradition practiced in the zurkaneh of Iran. British colonialists first came across these eastern artefacts in India however, hence the name. The 'Indian clubs' became exceedingly popular back in the UK, especially during the health craze of the Victorian era. In a book written in 1866, by an American sports enthusiast, S.D. Kehoe, it was stated that 'as a means of physical culture, the Indian Clubs stand pre-eminent among the varied apparatus of Gymnastics now in use.' He had visited England in 1861, and was so impressed with the sport that he began to manufacture and sell clubs to the American public in 1862. They were used by military cadets and upper class ladies alike, and even appeared as a gymnastic event at the 1904 and 1932

Olympics. Their popularity began to wane in the 1920s however, with the growing predilection for organised sports. The modern juggling club was inspired by the 'Indian club' though; first repurposed for juggling by DeWitt Cook in the 1800s. He taught his step son, Claude Bartram to juggle with them, who later went on to form the first 'club juggling act'. Today, their popularity has been revived somewhat, by fitness enthusiasts who that they are a far safer means of excising, rather than the traditional 'free weight regimens'. Nostalgic replicas of the original clubs are still manufactured, as well as modern engineering updates to the concept, such as the Clubbell.

EDWARD B. WARMAN.

WARMAN'S INDIAN CLUB SYSTEM

✿

ONE CLUB

✿

GENERAL DIRECTIONS

Grasp the club firmly, but easily, the little finger resting against the knob. As these exercises are intended for physical development and not for the purpose of displaying "fancy" or "snake movements"—very good in their way and for the purpose designed—it is advisable and necessary that the knob of the club should never slip to the thumb and forefinger; neither should the thumb extend up the handle of the club. Place the idle arm at the side, with the back of the fingers resting gracefully against the side of the body. Do not allow the club to wabble. When a movement is made requiring the arm to be extended, hold the club firmly, yet as gracefully as if it were a part of that extension. Imagine that you are standing between perfect circles at right angles with each other—large and small on either side; large in front and small behind. The clubs should follow these lines perfectly in all the small circles and sweeps.

Be satisfied to practice with one club until all the single moves have been mastered; the double moves will then be more readily attained, as they are combinations of the single.

Practice each move separately, as shown in the illustration of the same. Learn the *name* of each move, and it will be helpful, inasmuch as it is suggestive.

Do not be ambitious to handle heavy clubs. Judicious practice regularly taken with a pair of *light* clubs will prove more beneficial than spasmodic or overwork with *heavy* clubs. Stand firmly, but not rigidly. Place the feet in as graceful and comfortable a position as the nature of the movement will allow. Do not quite touch the heels, nor place them too far apart, when facing an audience.

POSITION.

Place the club in the hands, as shown in POSITION. Toss the club a little higher than the head, placing the left hand against the side of the body, the back of the fingers touching the body. Pass the right hand back of the head at the right side, and allow the club to drop and form a complete small circle back of the head, which I designate as the *small inward*. Follow this movement with a full sweep of the arm in front toward the left side, bringing it up on the right to make *two* small inwards, etc., thus forming Fig. 1.

FIG. 1.

Inward—Right—Small circle inward—Sweep in front (three times)

CHANGE—By halting the club, just as it sweeps up the right side, a little higher than the shoulder, and reverse the movement.

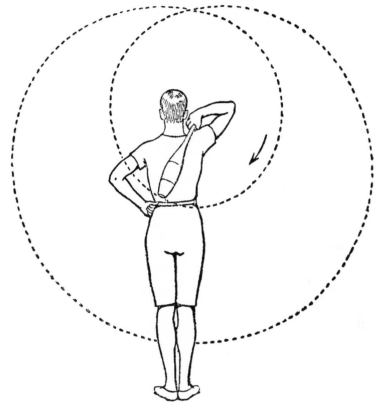

FIG. 2.

OUTWARD—RIGHT.

1. Small circle outward—Sweep in front.
2. "   "   "   "   "   "
3. "   "   "   "   "   "

CHANGE—By passing the club to the left hand just as it sweeps up toward the left side the third.time. When a little higher than the shoulder, let it fall to a small outward circle.

FIG. 3.

OUTWARD—LEFT.

1. Small circle outward—Sweep in front.
2. "   "   "   "   "   "
3. "   "   "

CHANGE—By omitting the third sweep outward, but instead drop the club in front of the face, following with a full sweep inward, bringing up the club on the left side and making a small inward circle.

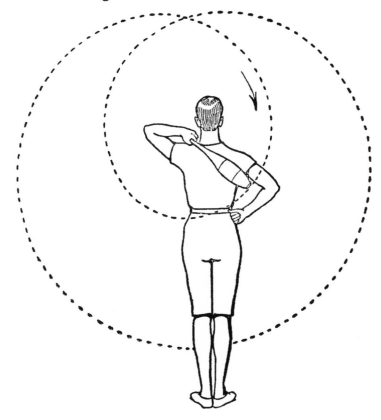

FIG. 4.

INWARD—LEFT.

1. Small circle inward—Sweep in front.
2. "   "   "   "   "   "
3. "   "   "   "   "   "

CHANGE—By halting the club when it sweeps up the left side the third time, poising it at *Poise 1,* as shown in the illustration.   Let it fall as if to make an outward, but instead of making a full circle, halt it at *Poise 2,* and then drop it in front of the face.

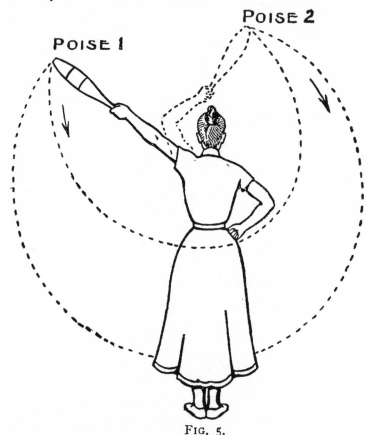

FIG. 5.

POISE—DROP. LEFT.

Poise at 1—Poise at 2—Drop in front of the face.

     "   "   "   "   "   "   "   "

     "   "   "   "   "   "   "   "

Change—By poising again at *Poise 1,* reversing the movement to a small outward; then sweep it in front, taking it up with the right hand and halting it at *Poise 1* on the right side. Let it fall as if to make an outward; but instead of making a full circle, halt it at *Poise 2,* and then drop it in front of the face.

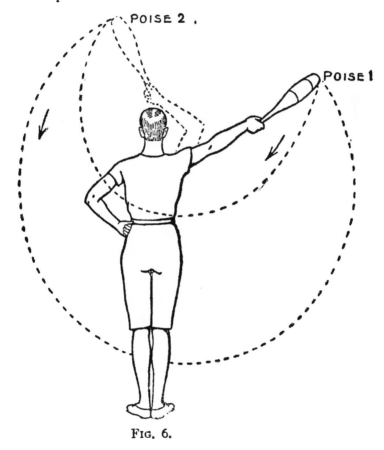

FIG. 6.

POISE—DROP. RIGHT.

Poise at 1—Poise at 2—Drop in front of the face (three times)

CHANGE—By poising again at *Poise 1,* and reversing the movement to a small outward; then sweep it in front and take it up with the left hand to *Poise 1,* left (as shown in Fig. 5); reverse it to a small outward, and pass it from hand to hand after each small outward.

FIG. 7.

ALTERNATING OUTWARD.

Outward—Right—Sweep. Outward—Left—Sweep.

CHANGE—By taking the club again in the right hand as if to make a fourth outward, but instead make a small inward, passing it quickly behind the head to the left hand, which should be in position to grasp the club without stopping its motion. It will drop into a small outward circle with the left hand. Sweep it out and front, pass it again to the right hand.

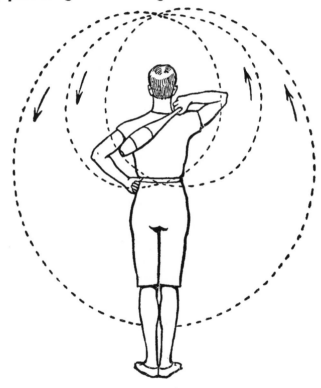

FIG. 8.

LARGE WHEEL—LEFT.

Inward—Right.　Outward—Left.　Sweep.
　　"　　　　　"　　　　　"　　　　"　　　　"
　　"　　　　　"　　　　　"　　　　"　　Drop.

CHANGE—By omitting the last sweep with the left hand; drop the club in front of the face, giving a full sweep inward, then small inward with left hand, thus reversing the movement.

FIG. 9.

LARGE WHEEL—RIGHT.

Inward—Left. Outward—Right. Sweep.

" " " " "

" " " " Drop.

CHANGE—By again omitting the outward sweep with right hand, drop the club in front of the face, giving a full sweep inward, thus reversing the movement, making only small circles.

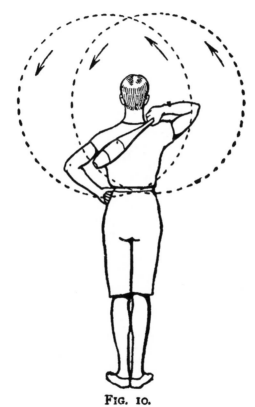

FIG. 10.

SMALL WHEEL—LEFT.

Inward—Right.	Outward—Left.	Avoid Sweep.
" "	" "	" "
" "	" "	Drop.

CHANGE—By dropping the club in front of the face with the left hand, following with a full sweep to inward left, thus reversing the movement.

It will be observed that, in making the small wheels, the sweeps are omitted, thus distinguishing between the large and small wheels.

FIG. 11.

SMALL WHEEL—RIGHT.

Inward—Left.	Outward—Right.	Avoid Sweep.
" "	" "	" "
" "	" "	Drop and Poise.

CHANGE—By again dropping the club in front of the face with the right, giving a full sweep inward; but, as the club comes up, halt it at *Poise 1,* swing it to *Poise 2,* and drop in front of the face, bringing it to an inward. Sweep it in front and halt it again at *Poise 1.*

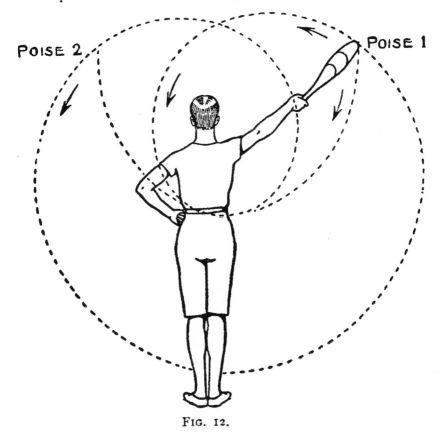

FIG. 12.

POISE—DROP—INWARD. RIGHT.
Poise at 1—Poise at 2—Drop—Inward—Sweep.
"   "   "   "   "   "   "
"   "   "   "   "   "   Pass over

CHANGE—By passing the club to the left hand, making the change back of the head. Pass from the last small inward circle with the right hand to a small outward with the left. Drop the club in front of the face and sweep it up to *Poise 1*, drop it back of the head to *Poise 2*, and then drop it in front of the face, and bring it to an inward. Sweep it in front, and halt it again at *Poise 1*.

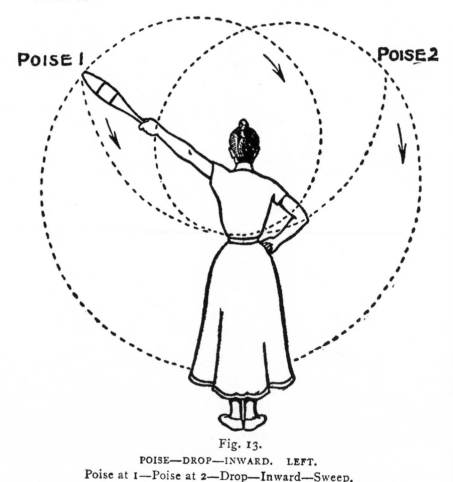

POISE 1

POISE 2

Fig. 13.

POISE—DROP—INWARD. LEFT.

Poise at 1—Poise at 2—Drop—Inward—Sweep.
   "   "   "   "   "   "   "
   "   "   "   "   "   "   Pass over

CHANGE—By passing the club to the right hand, making the change back of the head, going from a small inward left to a small outward right. Drop the club in front of the face and sweep it to an inward right, passing it directly back to the left hand—making the change back of the head—and making a drop and inward left.

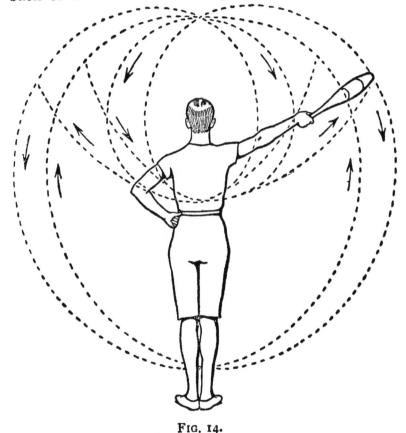

FIG. 14.

ALTERNATING DROP AND INWARD.

Drop—Sweep—Inward—Over. Drop—Sweep—Inward—Over.
  "   "   "   "   "   "   "   "
  "   "   "   Turn the body to the left.

CHANGE—By turning the body to the left just as the club is completing the last small inward circle. Keep the arm bent, and make a wrist circle at the side. Keep a firm hold on the club, not allowing the knob to slip to the thumb and forefinger.

FIG. 15.

SMALL SIDE.

Small side-circle. 1-2-3.

CHANGE—By extending the arm upward and forward, making a large circle at the side without bending the arm.

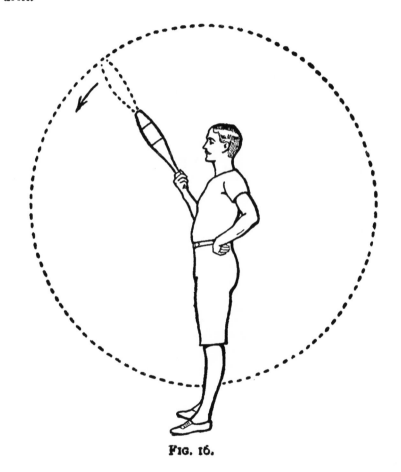

FIG. 16.

LARGE SIDE.
Large side-circles. 1-2-3.

CHANGE—By checking the club just as it passes the feet on the third downward stroke, and reversing the movement. Do not allow the club to wabble when checking it, nor the arm to bend when making the circle.

FIG. 17

REVERSE.

Large size—Reverse. 1–2–3.

CHANGE—As the club comes up in front on the third circle. When it is high enough, drop it to a *small* side, followed by a *large* side; then, as it is ready to descend as if to make a *second* large side, bring it diagonally to the left side with a full sweep, then back to the starting point of a large side, and make another large side-circle.

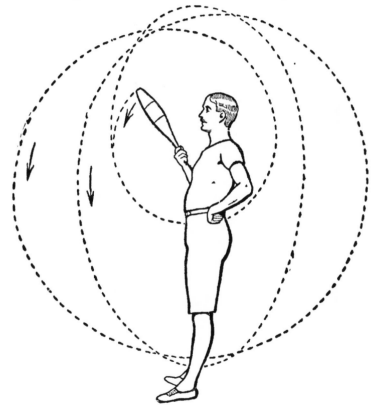

FIG. 18.

SIDE AND DIAGONAL.

One small—Large.   Diagonal—Large.
Two "   "   "   "
Three " and over.

CHANGE—At the close of the third small circle, by making a small inward and passing the club to the left hand, making the change back of the head. Make a small outward with the left, and when the club becomes vertical, drop it back to a small inward with the same hand, and when the club again becomes vertical, change the movement to a small side-circle.

FIG. 19.

SMALL SIDE.

Small side-circle. 1-2-3.

CHANGE—By extending the arm upward and forward, making a *large* circle at the side, without bending the arm.

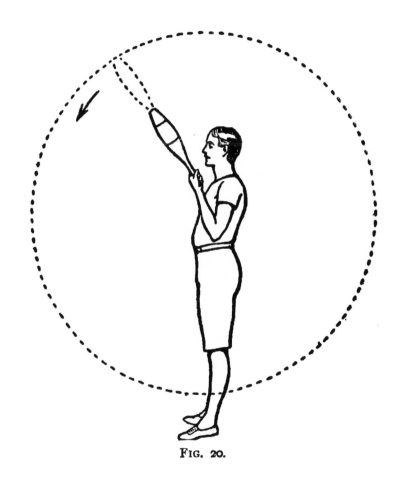

FIG. 20.

LARGE SIDE.
Large side-circle. 1-2-3.

CHANGE—By checking the club just as it passes the feet on the third downward stroke, and reversing the movement. Do not allow the club to wabble when checking it, nor the arm to bend in making the circle.

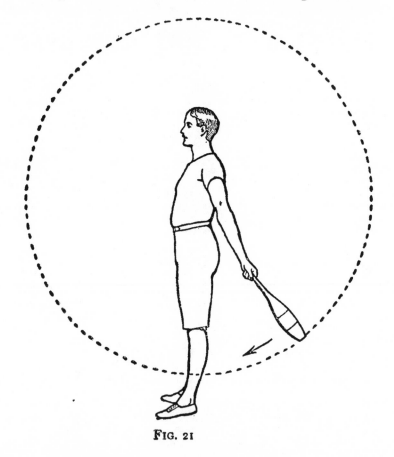

FIG. 21

REVERSE.

Large side—Reverse   1-2 3.

CHANGE—As the club comes up in front on the third circle. When it is high enough, drop it to a *small* side, followed by a *large* side; then, as it is ready to descend, as if to make a *second* large side, bring it diagonally to the right side with a full sweep; then back to the starting point of a *large side,* and make another large side-circle.

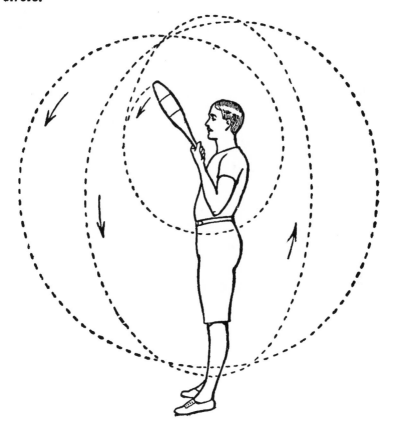

FIG. 22.

SIDE AND DIAGONAL.

1. Small—Large. Diagonal—Large.
2. "   "   "   "
3. "   and face front.

CHANGE—By extending the arm at the completion of the third small circle, as if to make a large side circle; then, just as the club is ready to sweep down, turn the body quickly back to the front position. Sweep the club in front, make a small outward with the left hand, and sweep it to the right. Place the right hand as shown in the illustration, and make small circles outside and inside the arm, keeping the arm extended as much as possible, and keep the club as *near* the arm as possible. *Keep the little finger next to the knob.*

Fig. 23—CHIN-KNOCKER.
Outside of arm—Inside of arm (three times each).
Sweep to the left hand.

CHANGE—By sweeping the club to the left hand and making a small outward with the left. Place the hand, as shown in the illustration, and make small circles outside and inside the arm, keeping the arm extended as much as possible; also keep the club moving as *near* the arm as possible. Do not let the knob of the club slip to the thumb and forefinger.

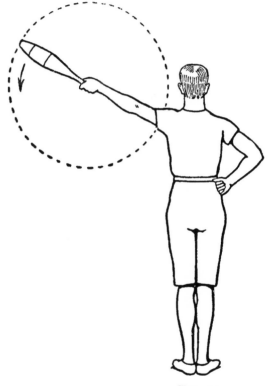

FIG. 24.

CHIN-KNOCKER.
Outside of arm—Inside of arm (three times each).
Sweep to right hand.

CHANGE—By small outward and sweep with left hand, carrying the club to the right side by the right hand, until the hand is straight with the shoulder, as seen in the illustration. Grasp the club firmly, and hold it in an upright position. Without *raising, lowering* or *bending* the arm the *slightest*, lay the club on the arm, then raise it and extend it till it is perfectly straight. Throughout this entire exercise the arm should not move nor bend at the elbow.

FIG. 25.

THE LEVER.

Upright—On the arm—Straight out.
    "   "   "   "
    "   "   "   "
        "   and toss to outward.

CHANGE—By tossing the club to a small outward, and sweep it to the left hand; stop the hand as soon as it is even with the shoulder, and place the club in an upright position. Lay the club on the arm without bending the arm at the elbow. Raise the club without moving the arm, and extend it until it is perfectly straight, as shown in the illustration.

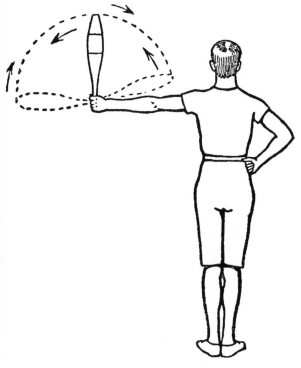

FIG. 26.

THE LEVER.

Upright—On the arm—Straight out.
"   "   "   "
"   "   "   "
"   "   and toss to outward

CHANGE—By tossing the club to a small outward.　Do not make a sweep, but just as the club completes the small circle, reverse it to a small inward.　Then, just as the club is upright, make a small side-circle, and when the club is again upright, make a small **inward,** thus alternating *small inwards* and *small sides.*

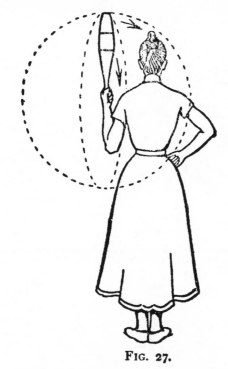

FIG. 27.

INWARD AND SIDE.

Small inward—Small side.

"   "   "   "

"   "   "   "

"   "   and over to the right.

CHANGE—By passing the club back of the head to the right hand. Make a small outward with the right hand, then reverse it to a small inward, and, as it comes to an upright position, change it to a small side-circle, then back to a small inward; thus alternating *small sides* and *small inwards.*

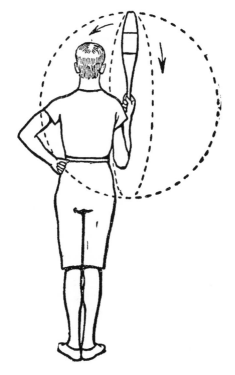

FIG. 28.

INWARD AND SIDE.

Small inward—Small side (three times each).
    "   "   and toss over the head, letting it drop gently in the left hand, as shown in Fig 1—position. This will give a graceful

FINISH.

CONDENSED FOR CONVENIENCE

❦

ONE CLUB

Presupposing that the pupil has become familiar with all the movements; *i.e.*, with the necessary *details* in the learning of each, I present herewith my system of exercises in a *condensed* form, as a reminder to the individual, or as an aid to the teacher in calling the movements to a class.

The order of exercises, and the number of movements of each, are the same as I use for my classes in their public exhibitions.

On the rostrum, at the close of my lecture on *"Scientific Physical Training, or the Care of the Body,"* I aim not only to entertain, but to exemplify the principles set forth in my lecture, by giving, in appropriate costume, my entire system of Indian-club exercises—the clubs weighing eight pounds each.

As a rule, I do not advocate the use of heavy clubs; but these, to me, do not seem heavy, having had them in use—privately and publicly—for thirty years.

My plan of work is on the principle of "cumulative strength"—the only *true* principle. Hence I advise the use of one club throughout the entire system of exercises; then rest a moment before swinging the two clubs. Rest again, if desirable, at the close of the "windmill," before concluding the entire system.

By so doing I find no difficulty in closing the evening's entertainment by a few movements with *both clubs* (16 lbs.) *in one hand.*

By adhering to these suggestions, *invigoration* will take the place of *exhaustion*. Be patient in well doing.

ONE CLUB.

No. 1. Inward Right—one.
     "   "   two.
     "   "   three.

No. 2. Outward Right—one.
     "   "   two.
     "   "   three.

No. 3. Outward Left—one.
     "   "   two.
     "   "   three. **Drop.**

No. 4. Inward Left—one.
     "   "   two.
     "   "   three.

No. 5. Poise and Drop—Left. 1-2-3.
No. 6. Poise and Drop—Right. 1-2-3.
No. 7. Outward Right—Outward Left.
     "   "   "   "
     "   "   "   "

No. 8. Large Wheel—to the Left. 1-2-3. Drop and reverse.
No. 9. Large Wheel—to the Right. 1-2-3. Drop and reverse.
No. 10. Small Wheel—to the Left. 1-2-3. Drop and reverse.
No. 11. Small Wheel—to the Right. 1-2-3. Drop and Poise.
No. 12. Poise—Drop—Inward Right. 1-2-3. Over.
No. 13. Poise—Drop—Inward Left. 1-23. Over.

No. 14. Drop—Inward Right—Over.
                 Drop—Inward Left—Over.
       Drop—Inward Right—Over.
                 Drop—Inward Left—Over.
       Drop—Inward Right—Turn.

No. 15. Small Side—Right. 1-2-3.

No. 16. Large Side—Right. 1-2-3.

No. 17. Reverse. 1-2-3.

No. 18. Small—Large—Diagonal—Large.
       2 "   "   "   "
       3 "   Change to left hand.

No. 19. Small Side—Left. 1-2-3.

No. 20. Large Side—Left. 1-2-3.

No. 21. Reverse. 1-2-3.

No. 22. Small—Large—Diagonal—Large.
       2 "   "   "   "
       3 "   Turn. Change to right.

No. 23. Chin-knocker—Right. 1-2-3.

No. 24. Chin-knocker—Left. 1-2-3.

No. 25. Lever—Right. 1-2-3.

No. 26. Lever—Left. 1-2-3.

No. 27. Inward and Small Side—Left. 1-2-3.

No. 28. Inward and Small Side—Right. 1-2-3.

Finish by tossing the club over the head, dropping it gently into the left hand.

TWO CLUBS

❧

GENERAL DIRECTIONS

When the clubs fall parallel in the same direction, they should drop simultaneously, and should not be separated from each other any greater distance *during* the movement than when the movement *began*.

With the single exception of a "follow" movement (the windmill, Fig. 12) both clubs should drop with the same impulse, even though they are making different movements. The slightest variation from this rule will destroy the gracefulness and beauty of the swinging.

When facing front, avoid turning the body from side to side, except in Fig. 1. Practice before a mirror, in order that every movement of the club may be seen while facing front. This will teach one to look at his audience, instead of turning his head and watching the clubs. Master your clubs instead of allowing them to master you.

Take position by pointing the two clubs to the left, as shown in the illustration. Keep the palms of the hands up in order to steady the clubs. Toss both clubs up and out, sweeping them down in front of the body, and bringing them up to left side. Avoid angles. Toss them out and bring them in as if describing an arc of a circle.

N. B.—To take up the clubs artistically—which cannot be done until all of the movements shall have been learned—see page 68.

FIG. I.

POINT.

Point left—Sweep.   Point right—Sweep (three times each).
    "   "   Halt.

CHANGE—By halting at position and making a small outward with the left, and a full sweep with the right; both clubs dropping simultaneously. The club in the right hand makes a large revolution, while the one in the left makes a small one.

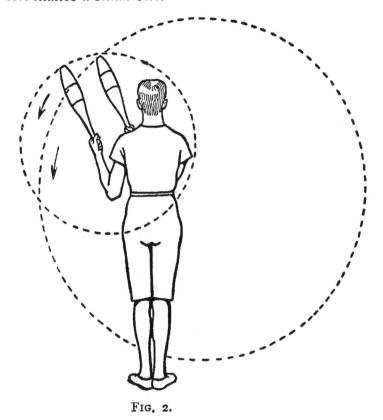

FIG. 2.

SMALL LEFT—LARGE RIGHT.

Small Wheel—left hand.   Large Wheel—right hand.

CHANGE—By sweeping both clubs in front and bringing them up on the right side, and halting them in position of point right.   Make a small outward with the
right hand, and a full sweep with the left, both clubs
falling simultaneously.

FIG. 3.

SMALL RIGHT.   LARGE LEFT.

Small Wheel—right hand.   Large Wheel—left hand.
"   "   "   "   "   "   "   "
"   "   "   "   "   "   "   "

CHANGE—By sweeping the clubs back to the left side and halting them a second, making a small outward with the left and a full sweep with the right. Sweep them both to the right side and halt only long enough to make a small outward with the right and a full sweep with the left; thus alternating the movement from side to side.

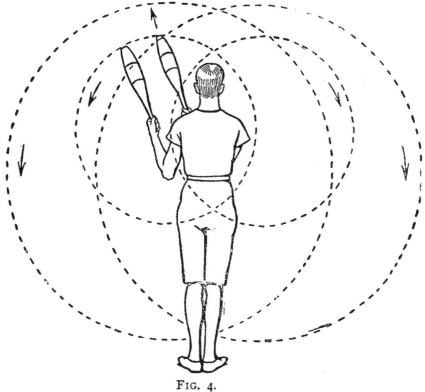

FIG. 4.

ALTERNATE.

Small left—Large right—Sweep.   Small right—Large left—Sweep.
" " " " " " " " " "
" " " " " " " " " "

CHANGE—By sweeping the clubs back to the left side and halting the club in the left hand at poise 1; but pass the right club up in front of the face and push it back of the head, letting it drop as if to make an inward. Instead of making a small circle, push it to the right, as shown in the illustration. As the right club drops behind the head, the left club sweeps in front toward the right side. The clubs now change position—the left club is pushed back of the head, and the right club sweeps in front.

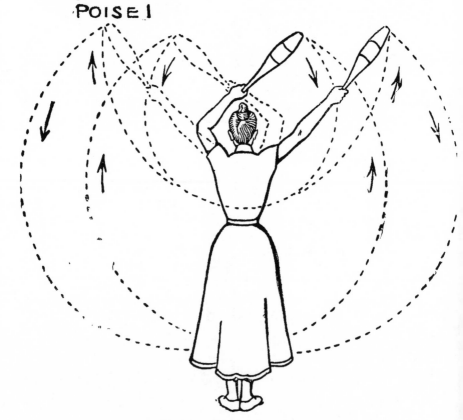

POISE 1

FIG. 5—BACKWARD DROP.

Backward drop—right—push. Backward drop—left—push.

CHANGE—By halting the left club at poise 1; swing it to poise 2; and drop it in front of the face. While this is being done the right club sweeps back on the circle in front, and halts at poise 1 on the right side, then to poise 2, and drops in front of the face; thus making the regular poise and drop with each hand.

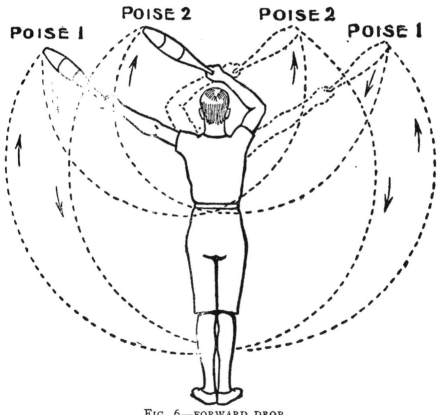

FIG. 6—FORWARD DROP.

Poise and drop—Left.   Poise and drop—Right.

CHANGE—By halting the clubs a second when they are on the left side. Turn the left club to an outward, while the right club passes down in front and sweeps up on the right side, making a small inward and push—as in the backward drop. It then sweeps down in front and is pushed back of the head, making a backward drop and push, while the left club is making an outward.

FIG. 7—OUTWARD LEFT—BACKWARD DROP.

Outward left—Sweep. Backward drop and push—Right.
(Three times each).

CHANGE—By converting the backward push and drop of the right club, to an outward and sweep. When the club is pushed *right* the third time, instead of dropping it in front, turn it immediately to an outward. The left club makes no change but continues making the outward and sweep.

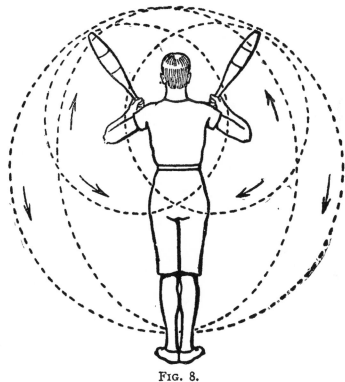

FIG. 8.
ALTERNATING OUTWARD.

Outward left—Sweep.   Outward right—Sweep.

CHANGE—By halting both clubs a second, just as the
right club closes the third small outward.   Reverse it
to a small inward, followed by a full sweep.   The left
club also reverses its movement, making a sweep, followed by a small inward.   One club is making an inward while the other is making a sweep.

FIG. 9.

ALTERNATING INWARD.

Inward right—Sweep.   Inward left—Sweep.

   "   "   "   "   "   "

   "   "   "   Both clubs left side.

CHANGE—By making a small outward left, and a full sweep with the right; *i.e.,* what is known as small left, large right. Sweep both clubs in front at the same time, and bring them up on the right side, and sweep them up, over and back of the head, making small circles, both clubs parallel, as shown in the illustration.

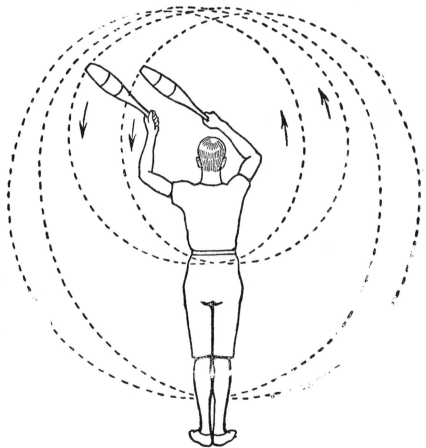

FIG. 10—SMALL CIRCLES—BACK.
One small circle—Sweep. Two small circles—Sweep.
Three small circles—Change.

CHANGE—By making an *extra* small circle with the left hand while the right sweeps in front. The right hand passes back to a small inward, while the left hand sweeps in front. By the time the small inward is finished with the right hand, the left will be in place for a small outward. The clubs now join, and make another double circle back of the head.

FIG. 11—LEFT—RIGHT—BOTH.

Small left—Sweep.	Small right—Sweep.	Small—Both.
" " "	" " "	2 " "
" " "	" " "	3 " "

CHANGE—By pushing the left club up and out from the shoulder, while hastening the right in front, and making a full sweep, till—without halting either club—the right club is exactly opposite the left, just after the right passes the feet—both arms extended.   The clubs should now follow each other, but neither *catch* the other. The right hand makes an inward and sweep, while the left is following with a sweep and outward.

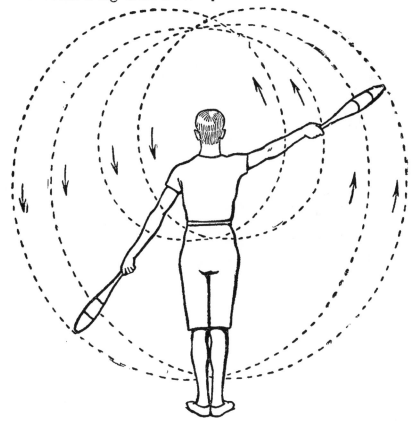

FIG. 12—THE WINDMILL.

Inward right—Outward left—Sweep—Swe**
    "   "   "   "   "   "
    ".   "   "   omit sween

CHANGE—By slowing up on the left till the right catches it. Sweep both clubs in front and then back of the head, as shown by position of clubs in Fig. 10. Continue the small inward circles with the right hand, but shift the position of the left a trifle forward, making small side circles. Both clubs should fall and rise at the same time, each crossing the track of the other. Swing them so that the circles are at right angles.

FIG. 13—SIDE AND INWARD—LEFT.
Small side—Left.   Small inward—Right (three times each).

CHANGE—By quickly shifting the clubs to the *right* side, making a small inward with the left, and a small side with the right.

FIG. 14.

SIDE AND INWARD—RIGHT.

Small side—Right.   Small inward—Left.

" " "   " " "

" " "   " " "

· CHANGE.—By shifting the clubs back to the left side, and then back to the right, continuing the same movement, but alternating from side to side.

FIG. 15.

ALTERNATE.

Side and inward—Left.   Side and inward—Right.

CHANGE—By bringing the clubs to a perpendicular poise on each side of the head. Make a small inward with the right, then a small inward with the left; again with the right, and again with the left. Sweep the right in front of the face, then the left, and bring them up to repeat the small inwards with each.

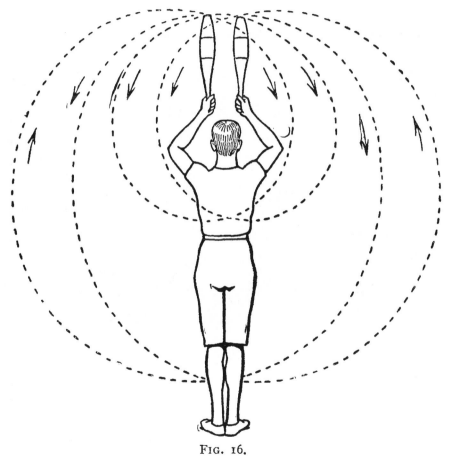

FIG. 16.

RIGHT—LEFT—RIGHT—LEFT—SWEEP—SWEEP.
Inward right-Inward left-Inward right-Inward left-Sweep-Sweep.
"   "   "   "   "   "   "   "   "   "
"   "   "   "   "   "   "   " omit sweep.

Change—By omitting the sweep the third time. At the conclusion of the small circles, bring the clubs again to a perpendicular poise on each side of the head, and make small side-circles; both clubs falling and rising simultaneously.

FIG. 17.

SMALL SIDES.

Small side—Right.			Small side—Left.			Together.
"	"	"	"	"	"	"
"	"	"	"	"	"	"

CHANGE—By bringing the clubs again to a perpendicular poise on each side of the head. Make small inwards with each hand at the *same time,* the clubs crossing each other at the handles.

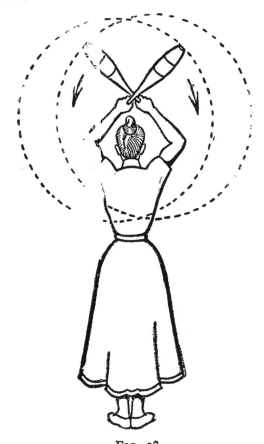

FIG. 18.

SMALL INWARDS.

Small inward—Right. Small inward—Left. Together.

CHANGE—By sweeping both clubs in front of the face at the same time, crossing each other above and below in the circle. Keep the arms as fully extended as possible.

FIG. 19.

INWARD SWEEPS.

Sweep inward—Right.   Sweep inward—Left.   Together.

"   "   "   "   "   "   "

"   "   "   "   "   "   "

CHANGE—By bringing the clubs again to a perpendicular poise on each side of the head, and then unite the last three moves in one; *i.e.,* giving them in succession—one of each.

FIG. 20—SIDE—INWARD—SWEEP.

Small sides—Small inwards—Sweeps.

" " " " "

" " " " "

" " change.

CHANGE—By bringing the clubs again to a perpendic‑
ular poise, and swing them to small circles toward the
left, as shown by position of clubs in Fig. 10. Then
turn the body quickly to the left—without moving the
left foot. Make small side-circles once. Sweep the
clubs together, bringing them up on the *right* side. Turn
the body right—without moving the right foot, and
make small side-circles once. Sweep the clubs back
to the left side and repeat. Both clubs should fall to‑
gether—only one club being visible to any one sitting
directly opposite.

FIG. 21—SMALL SIDE—LEFT AND RIGHT.
Small side—Left—Sweep.   Small side—Right—Sweep.

CHANGE—By halting the left club as it points up till the right club points down. Instead of the clubs falling simultaneously, they now fall successively, in the same direction.

FIG. 22.
ALTERNATE.

Small sides.	Down—Right.	Down—Left
"	"	" "
"	"	" "

CHANGE—By halting the right club when it points up, till the left club also points up. Continue the small side-circle *forward*, with the *left* hand, but *reverse* the small side-circle with the *right* hand. Again both clubs fall simultaneously, though in *opposite* directions.

FIG. 23.

REVERSE.

Small sides.	Forward—Left.	Reverse—Right.
"	"	" "
"	"	" "

CHANGE—By halting both clubs when vertical, make *small sides* and sweep to the left. Turn the body to the left without moving the left foot. Make small sides as soon as the clubs come up on the left side; then make small circles again, but pass both clubs *inside* the arms; then again small circles *outside;* then thrust both clubs under the arms, as shown in the illustration. Then toss the clubs up for small circles again. Both clubs fall inside or outside, as the case may be, *at same time.*

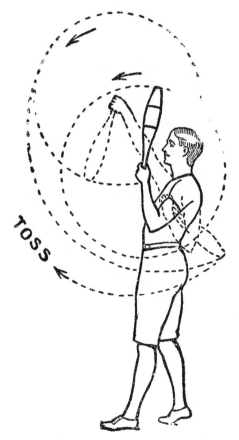

FIG. 24—DOUBLE CHIN KNOCKER.
Small circles—Outside—Inside—Outside—Under. Toss.
(Three times each.)

Change—By sweeping the clubs in front—now facing front. Check the right club when the arm and club are perfectly horizontal. Push the left club back of the head and make a small inward, three times, while holding the right hand and club perfectly quiet. Sweep the left club in front, make a poise and drop, and, *as* it drops, sweep the right club down with it.

POISE

FIG. 25—RIGHT HORIZONTAL.
Horizontal—Right.   Inward 1—Left.
 "   2   "
 "   3   " and sweep.
Poise and drop—Left.   Sweep both.

CHANGE—By sweeping the clubs up to the left side, holding the *left* arm horizontal, and passing the *right* club back of the head. Make three small inward circles with the right hand, then sweep in front of the face, and make a poise and drop with the right hand.

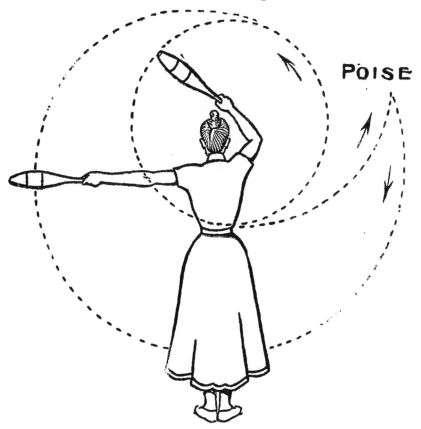

POISE

FIG. 26—LEFT HORIZONTAL.

Horizontal—Left. Inward 1—Right.
" 2 "
" 3 " and sweep.
Poise and drop—Right—Sweep both.

Change—By sweeping the clubs to a small circle back of the head, as shown by the position of the clubs in Fig. 10. Turn the body *squarely* to the left, the weight on both feet. Make a small side-circle with the left hand, while the right makes a large side-circle. Then make a small side-circle with the *right* hand, and a *large* side-circle with the left. Both clubs should fall with the same impulse—the one making a large circle, while the other makes a small.

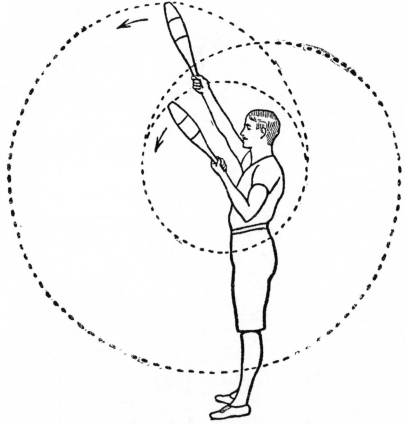

FIG. 27—SHOULDER BRACE.

Small left—Large right.   Small right—Large left.
"   "   "   "   "   "   "   "
"   "   "   "   change

CHANGE—By checking the large side-circle, with the right hand, just as the club has passed a short distance back of the feet.   At the same time extend the left arm and club up and forward—pointing exactly opposite the right.   Slip the right foot a little back of the left—the momentum of the club on the downward sweep will aid you.   With a quick but strong impulse sweep both clubs at once in opposite directions—the left arm makes a large circle forward, the right arm a large circle reversed.   Keep the arms *unbent* and close to the body.

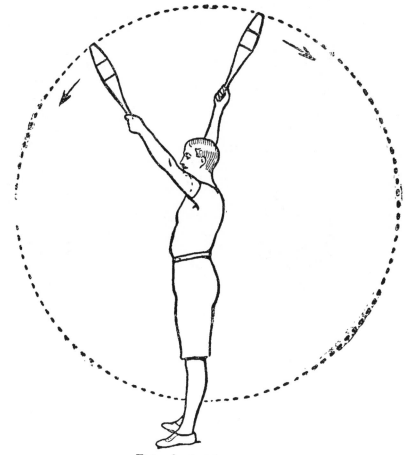

FIG. 28—LARGE REVERSE.

Left and Right—opposite (repeat three times.)

CHANGE—By halting the right club as it sweeps up in front on the third reverse. Let it fall to a *small side*. Check the left club as it passes the feet the third time, and bring it up in front with a sweep. It will reach there in time to join the right club as it makes a second small side-circle. Join them (both making a *small side*), sweep them to the front (turning the body front), and pass them back of the head, making small circles back, as shown by position of clubs in Fig. 10. Pass directly to the *windmill*, and add small side alternates (Fig. 22).

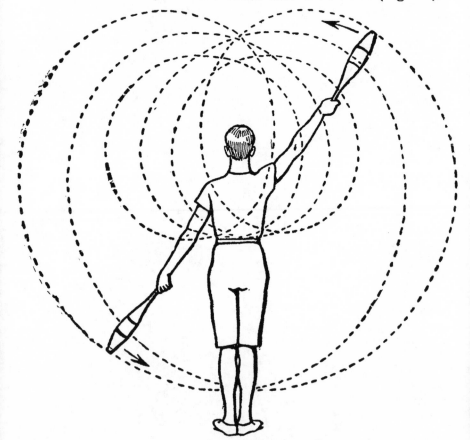

FIG. 29—WINDMILL—ALTERNATE.

Inward right—Outward left—Small side right—Small side left—
Sweep right. Sweep left. Repeat three times. Sweep *both*.

THE FINISH

Halt the right club when completing the third small alternate, till the left club comes up on the third small circle. Sweep both in front with one impulse, and pass them back over the head to a small circle, as shown by the position of the clubs in Fig. 10. Follow this with a small side-circle (Fig. 21). Pass the clubs gracefully under the arms (Fig. 24). Keep them there till you have made your bow and exit.

TWO CLUBS

ॐ

TO TAKE UP BOTH CLUBS ARTISTICALLY

Face front.   Stand between the clubs.   Fold the
arms.   With the first note of the music unfold the arms,
raise the hands above the head and sweep them down
to the side.   Bend the body, take the clubs with suffi-
cient impulse to sweep them a short distance back.
Straighten the body, and this will give the clubs an impulse forward.   Sweep them up high enough in front
to make small side-circles (Fig. 17), then small circles
back of the head (Fig. 10), then, turning the body
quickly to the left, make small side-circles (Fig. 21),
halting them in position of Fig. 1—two clubs.

I herewith present my *system* of exercises:

CONDENSED FOR CONVENIENCE—TWO CLUBS.

No. 1. Point Left. Right—Left.
     "   "
     "   "

No. 2. Small left—Large right. 1-2-3. Sweep.
No. 3. Small right—Large left. 1-2-3. Sweep.
No. 4. Alternate. Left—Right.
     "   "
     "   "   sweep.

No. 5. Backward drop. Right—Left.
      "   "
      "   "

No. 6. Forward drop. Left—Right.
     "   "
     "   "

No. 7. Outward left—Backward drop, right.
    "   "
    "   "

No. 8. Alternating outward. Left—Right.
      "   "
      "   "

No. 9. Alternating inward. Right—Left.
      "   "
       "   sweep.

No. 10. Small back circles. 1—Sweep.
         2   "
         3   change.

No. 11. Left—Right—Both 1
   "   "   "   2
   "   "   "   3   change.

No. 12. Windmill. 1-2-3.

No. 13. Side and inward—Left side. 1-2-3.

No. 14. Side and inward—Right side. 1-2-3.

No. 15. Alternate. Left—Right.
     "   "
     "   "

No. 16.   Right—Left—Right—Left—Sweep—Sweep
    "   "   "   "   "   "
    "   "   "   "   Halt.

No. 17. Small sides. 1-2-3.

No. 18. Small inwards. 1-2-3.

No. 19. Double inward sweeps. 1-2-3.

No. 20. Small sides—Inwards—Sweeps.
    "   "   "
    "   "   "
    "   Turn.

No. 21. Small sides, left—one.   Small sides, right—one.
    "   " two.   "   " two.
    "   " three.   "   " three.

No. 22. Alternate. Right—Left.
     "   "
     ..   ..

No. 23. Reverse. 1-2-3. Sweep to left side.

No. 24. Out—In—Out—Under. Toss.
    "   "   "   "   "
    "   "   "   "   "
    " and sweep.

No. 25. Right—Horizontal.
   Left—Inward. 1-2-3. Sweep.
   "   Poise and drop.
   Take it along (the right club).

No. 26. Left—Horizontal.

       Right—Inward. 1-2-3 Sweep.

         "   Poise and drop.

              Take it along (the left club). Sweep—turn.

No. 27. Shoulder brace. Left—Right.

                  "   "

               " reverse.

No. 28. Large reverse. 1-2-3.

No. 29. Windmill and alternate. 1-2-3.

Pass the clubs under the arms, and make your bow and exit.

31187652R00049

Made in the USA
Lexington, KY
17 February 2019